A LIVING ROOM RETREAT

A Living Room Retreat

REVISED EDITION

HELEN CECILIA SWIFT, SND DE N.

ALBA·HOUSE   NEW·YORK

SOCIETY OF ST. PAUL. 2187 VICTORY BLVD., STATEN ISLAND. NEW YORK 10314

ST PAULS

Library of Congress Cataloging-in-Publication Data

Swift, Helen.
  A living room retreat / Helen Cecilia Swift. — Rev. ed.
      p.   cm.
    ISBN 0-8189-0687-1
    1. Retreats. 2. Meditations. I. Title.
  BV5068.R4S94   1994
  269'.6 — dc20   93-39417
                                                        CIP

Produced and designed in the United States of America by the
Fathers and Brothers of the Society of St. Paul,
2187 Victory Boulevard, Staten Island, New York 10314,
as part of their communications apostolate.

ISBN: 0-8189-0687-1

Printing Information:

Current Printing - first digit   2   3   4   5   6   7   8   9   10

Year of Current Printing - first year shown

    1999 2000 2001 2002 2003 2004 2005 2006 2007

CONTENTS

Week Twelve
FOCUS ON BECOMING A FORERUNNER

FOREWORD TO REVISED EDITION

The first edition of this book was a response to the expressed desire of Christian women to enrich their prayer, to learn to pray with Scripture and to come together to share their faith life. Since then many thousands of women and men have grown spiritually and have experienced the value of community in their faith sharing.

The past fifteen years have also witnessed the proliferation of support groups to meet numerous human needs. As people experience some healing in these support groups, they express a desire to enrich their lives at a deeper level. They are looking for the sense of community they have come to value in the support group and also a deeper relationship with God and other Christians. This revised edition of the *Living Room Retreat* attempts to meet this need.

This revision follows the same basic format as the first edition, but the content of the meditations reflect some insights in theology that have developed over the past decade. There is greater emphasis on our interdependence with one another and with all of creation. Those who found spiritual growth through the first edition will profit again through prayer with these revised meditations.

INTRODUCTION

The purpose of this book is to present a process for getting in touch with God's action in your life and integrating your spiritual growth. Making this retreat with others allows you to appreciate your own faith journey and realize that you have the support of other Christians as you travel this way together. You will discover more meaning in your daily life as you see your relationship to all of creation. Through this process you will become more your true self: more human in the pattern of Jesus, quicker to respond with love to God, to your neighbor, to yourself and to all living things.

This book, of course, will not accomplish all that for you; no book can. What this volume offers is a framework through which you can let God reach you, together with a plan for allowing other people to enrich your reflections. It is a plan for a retreat — a withdrawal for a brief time each day from the pressures of life for quiet communion with God.

Unlike other retreats, this retreat will not require disrupting your life or setting aside your responsibilities for a lengthy period of time. It is planned to cover a span of 12 weeks, but all it asks of you is a commitment to spend at least 15 minutes in quiet prayer each day and, if at all possible, to meet each week with your group.

The meditations in these pages follow the

general pattern of the *Spiritual Exercises* of St. Ignatius Loyola, father of the modern retreat movement. While the lives of the saints testify that there is no single way leading to God, the test of time has proved the *Spiritual Exercises* a fruitful method for many people. However, Ignatius was a man of his time, and the psychology and theology underlying the *Exercises* fit his time rather than ours. Therefore, the *Exercises* must be adapted to new developments in psychology and new insights in theology.

Each week of the retreat follows a pattern. A brief introduction highlights certain concepts and presents some suggestions for prayer you will need to keep in mind during the week. Then follow five meditations, each based on a Scripture passage with a particular blessing to be desired. There are only five meditations for each week so that you can go back to the one which was most fruitful for you or try again the prayer that seemed to present difficulties.

Within the pattern for each week, the meditations allow enough flexibility for God to set the pace for your movement through the retreat. They are intended only to spark your prayer.

Praying the Meditations

God is always aware of us, breathing life and love into us at every moment, but we are not always aware of God. In prayer we attempt to become conscious of God's presence, to listen to God's voice within and respond from our hearts.

Prayer is always a gift, one that God desires to give to us. We can and should prepare to receive God's gift of prayer. You will find the following five steps helpful in your preparation for prayer:

1) *Relax.* Find a quiet place where you will not be disturbed. Take a position — sitting, reclining, kneeling — that is comfortable for you. Breathe slowly and deeply several times. Let the cares and concerns of the day fall away, quiet your mind and, without strain or tension, turn your thoughts to God.

2) *Realize* that you are always present to God. Let God's love and care be alive in you as you rest in the presence of your Creator.

3) *Read* slowly the Scripture passage given at the beginning of each meditation. If possible, read aloud so that your ears as well as your eyes take in the passage. Let this message from God into your heart. Then read the short meditation. You may want to go back and reread the Scripture in light of the points raised in the meditation.

4) *Ask* how God is speaking to your heart through this passage. Wait for a few minutes, quietly aware of God. If the passage leaves you dry, if it seems to have no meaning for you, read it again very slowly. Again wait quietly for God. If nothing happens, try another passage.

5) *Respond* to God. If a phrase or sentence attracts you (or possibly repels you in some way), tell God in your own words how you

feel about it. Use your feelings as the basis for a dialogue with the Father or with Jesus or with the Holy Spirit.

Keeping a Journal

As you pray each day, keep a note book handy and jot down significant points at the end of your prayer. Not only will the journal be helpful in sharing with others the fruits of your prayer; it will also help you to see more clearly the progress of your retreat. Some people keep prayer journals over the years and find it enlightening to read them from time to time. It is good to stand back and see how God has been acting in one's life.

After you have finished your prayer each day, reflect how you have met God in this prayer. The following questions may be helpful:

1) What was your mood at the beginning of prayer? Were you happy, sad, confident, worried, etc.?
2) Did your mood change during the prayer? Why — or why not?
3) Did you feel attracted by the subject of this meditation? Why?
4) Did you feel resistance to praying about this topic? Can you get in touch with the source of this resistance?
5) Do you feel that you really met God in this prayer?

6) What did God teach you today through prayer?

Do not feel that you must answer these questions one by one, after each day's prayer. They only suggest what might strike you. Your prayer is first of all a time for sharing with God. Do not be too concerned about the external structure of your prayer nor think ahead to what you will write in your notebook. You will only stop praying and miss God's tender, intimate presence.

A Plan for Sharing

You can certainly use this book for individual prayer. However, if you make the retreat alone, one important dynamic will be missing — the experience of Church. God relates to us not only as individuals, but as a community. In creating us, God has entrusted to each of us gifts for others. Other people can make an important contribution to your retreat in two ways:

1) They can help you prepare for each week's meditations. The more clearly you understand the focus of the meditations before entering into them, the better you will be able to hear what God is saying to you.
2) They can share with you — and you with them — the discoveries made in prayer during the previous week. The insight you find in prayer, however insignificant it may

seem to you, may be just the understanding someone else needs. Similarly, another may hold the sliver of insight that makes everything fall into place for you.

To make the best possible use of this book, therefore, you will need someone with whom to share it. If you are part of a discussion club or a prayer group, you already have a group of companions for the journey. If not, you may want to find someone to walk with you.

The ideal combination for a living room retreat is a group of 10-12 people. They might share an element of common experience, but that is not necessary.

Another possibility is to make the retreat with your spouse. Sincere, in-depth sharing once a week has a transforming effect on any marriage. Or you might move through the meditations in the company of a friend, perhaps using the telephone to share your insights and prepare for the coming week. Or your whole family could make the journey together. Some adjustments in the meditations may be necessary for children, but even the very young could participate in some way. Children often have fresh and thought-provoking viewpoints to express.

Choosing a Leader/Director for a Group

Leadership will surface in any group, but in a retreat a particular kind of leadership is called for: direction. The leader of a retreat should do more than keep a discussion on course or safeguard each person's opportunity to be heard. He or she must be sufficiently familiar with the program's thrust to explain the concepts underlying the meditations or answer questions as they arise. Support and encouragement when prayer seems dry is another function of the retreat director. For the director, familiarity with the Ignatian *Exercises* is helpful but not necessary.

The Group Meeting

People bonded by blood, marriage or close friendship seldom need elaborately structured meeting plans to facilitate sharing; they only need to get together for some time. The format suggested here is intended for larger, less naturally formed groups who do need structure. This pattern for sharing and preparation, however freely adapted, is the very heart of the retreat's communal dimension and should serve as a model for all companions on the journey.

An average group will need to set aside about two hours a week for 12 weekly group meetings. The purpose of the meetings is to share the experience of the past week and to prepare for the coming week.

The first and last meetings may be somewhat shorter. A group should take a brief time at the beginning of the first week to introduce themselves and share their hopes and expectations for the retreat, but most of that meeting will focus on preparation. The last meeting will only involve sharing and some prayer of closure.

Some suggestions for the director/facilitator are:

1) Begin each meeting promptly.
2) Create a prayerful atmosphere. Music, with or without singing, is helpful. Someone can then offer a short opening prayer.
3) Logically, the preparation for the next week should follow the sharing on the previous week, but experience has shown the wisdom of doing the preparation first. Otherwise, with some very articulate groups the preparation might be squeezed into the last few minutes.

   The director comments on the focus of the meditations for the following week and then gives some background on each of the meditations. A biblical commentary might provide some helpful insights but the director should take care not to present too many ideas. Leave God free to lead each retreatant.
4) Share the fruits of last week's prayer. Use the jottings in your journal to refresh your memory. Each one shares the responsibility for creating an accepting climate. Attentive, empathetic listening invites sharing without imposing pressure to speak. Listen not only to the words of others, but to the feelings being expressed. Then you can give to one another the assurance that each is unique and precious, a gift lovingly given and gratefully received.

Different Gifts

Our response to reality influences our prayer, and extroverts and introverts respond in different ways. Extroverts see the outer world as the primary reality. They are interested in people and events; they are more likely to discern God's presence in tangible things. Their prayer often focuses on this outer reality, expressing keen awareness of the Christian call to service.

Introverts, on the other hand, confront the reality of the inner world. It is in the silence of their hearts that they most often hear the voice of God. They enjoy quiet and, as they share their prayer, may sound more "prayerful" than extroverts. This does not mean one group prays better than the other, only that the style of their prayer is different.

Whatever the style, each person needs to tell his or her own story and, in the telling, become more aware of God's goodness, of God's action in life's events, of his uniquely personal call to spread his Kingdom in unity with Jesus. When you become more aware of God's part in your story — and more willing to allow him to direct its unfolding — the retreat will have achieved its goal.

Biblical Abbreviations

OLD TESTAMENT

Genesis	Gn	Nehemiah	Ne	Baruch	Ba
Exodus	Ex	Tobit	Tb	Ezekiel	Ezk
Leviticus	Lv	Judith	Jdt	Daniel	Dn
Numbers	Nb	Esther	Est	Hosea	Ho
Deuteronomy	Dt	1 Maccabees	1 M	Joel	Jl
Joshua	Jos	2 Maccabees	2 M	Amos	Am
Judges	Jg	Job	Jb	Obadiah	Ob
Ruth	Rt	Psalms	Ps	Jonah	Jon
1 Samuel	1 S	Proverbs	Pr	Micah	Mi
2 Samuel	2 S	Ecclesiastes	Ec	Nahum	Na
1 Kings	1 K	Song of Songs	Sg	Habakkuk	Hab
2 Kings	2 K	Wisdom	Ws	Zephaniah	Zp
1 Chronicles	1 Ch	Sirach	Si	Haggai	Hg
2 Chronicles	2 Ch	Isaiah	Is	Malachi	Ml
Ezra	Ezr	Jeremiah	Jr	Zechariah	Zc
		Lamentations	Lm		

NEW TESTAMENT

Matthew	Mt	Ephesians	Ep	Hebrews	Heb
Mark	Mk	Philippians	Ph	James	Jm
Luke	Lk	Colossians	Col	1 Peter	1 P
John	Jn	1 Thessalonians	1 Th	2 Peter	2 P
Acts	Ac	2 Thessalonians	2 Th	1 John	1 Jn
Romans	Rm	1 Timothy	1 Tm	2 John	2 Jn
1 Corinthians	1 Cor	2 Timothy	2 Tm	3 John	3 Jn
2 Corinthians	2 Cor	Titus	Tt	Jude	Jude
Galatians	Gal	Philemon	Phm	Revelation	Rv

A LIVING ROOM RETREAT

Week One
FOCUS ON YOU

The meditations of the first week give you an opportunity to reflect on your image of yourself. It may seem strange to begin a retreat by thinking and praying about yourself, but your retreat is meant to deepen your relationship with God. This relationship involves two persons, God and you. In order to understand and appreciate this relationship, it is important to get a clear understanding of both persons. This week the focus will be on you.

Some of the meditations suggest that you allow God to bring to memory incidents from your childhood and adolescence. These past moments and experiences are not lost but are still with you, either consciously or unconsciously. These are some of the elements that make you who you are today.

The meditations this week focus on positive aspects of your self-concept. These attempts to look at yourself as God sees you — lovable and loving — can have two effects. First, you begin to see some discrepancies between your image of yourself and God's. You may find it difficult to claim the good in yourself and rejoice with God in your goodness. Your very difficulty indicates some areas where progress is needed toward greater freedom. Second, trying to see yourself as

God sees you will help to bring about a closer correspondence of your self-image with God's concept of you. Other meditations during this retreat will aim at deepening both these graces.

Your image of yourself will influence how you look upon God. For example, if you are convinced of your lovableness, you can envision God as loving and caring. But if you have a negative self-image, you are more likely to imagine God as harsh and punishing.

Getting in touch with your image of yourself during this first week will help you notice any changes that take place in your self-concept as the retreat progresses. As you become conscious of these changes, reflect again on your image of God and look for alterations in your vision.

Before you begin each meditation, review the suggestions for prayer found in the introduction. At the end of prayer write in your journal anything you would like to remember for yourself or for group sharing next week.

HERE I AM, LORD

Read Mark 6:30-32.
Read slowly, trying to place yourself in the scene.
Blessing to be desired: generosity.

Jesus had sent the disciples out on their first mission with instructions to preach, anoint the sick and drive out demons (Mk 6:7-13). When they returned, two by two, they were bursting with news of all they had done.

Jesus invited them to come apart with him to share their experiences and rest after their journeys.

Jesus is inviting you now to come apart with him for a little time each day. Tell Jesus how you feel about this invitation. As you begin this ongoing retreat what expectations do you have? How do you desire God to bless you during this retreat?

Talk to Jesus about any difficulties you might encounter in making this retreat — a busy schedule, many responsibilities, finding a place of privacy and quiet. Spend some time telling him of your hopes, your expectations — even your fears — as you begin this retreat.

YOU ARE SPECIAL

Read Psalm 139:1-6, 13-14.
Blessing to be desired: a deep conviction
that you are very special to God.

God created you. What a simple but profound statement! The All-Holy One, by a special act of God's will made you. You are made in the image of God, so you too are a creator. You share in God's creative energies. How special you must be to God!

You are unique among the millions and millions of human beings God has created. You have a special place in God's vast universe for no one else can love and serve God in the same way you do. Look about you at the beauties of God's creation and ask all these creatures to join you in praising God for you are wonderfully made!

Spend some time rejoicing in your uniqueness and your specialness to God. Thank God for creating you just as you are.

HOW GOOD IS THE GOOD GOD!

Read Isaiah 49:15-16a.
Blessing to be desired: a
grateful heart.

God loves you with an unconditional love. As a loving parent, God loves you just as you are at this moment with no conditions or limits on love. God has cared for you and watched over you from the first moment of your life, showering you with tokens of love that are unique to you.

God is always present and active in your life. Even when you are not aware of God, the initial impulses moving you to think kind thoughts, to speak the honest word, to care and to love all come from God's goodness. Without God you could do nothing that is good — *nothing at all*!

Thank God as you recall how God has been active in your life — in the past, last week, yesterday. God's action moved you to do good and loving deeds so that you might share more abundantly in God's goodness. Offer your gratitude and praise to God.

GOD REJOICES OVER YOU

Read Zephaniah 3:14, 17.
*Blessing to be desired: a true love
of yourself.*

Some translations of Zephaniah 3:17 read: "God will dance with joy because of you." Can you imagine God being filled with joy because of your goodness and the love you give to others?

It is so easy when thinking of the past to allow negative memories to come to mind. Somehow it is easier to acknowledge failures and regret faults of the past rather than rejoice in the good.

Take some time now to look at the other side of your life. Walk slowly with God through the years looking at the many good and loving things you have done for others. Allow God to bring to your mind specific occasions, particular people — perhaps events and people you have not recalled for a long time. This is the way God sees you — your true self. Share God's joy — rejoice and be glad for you are a wonderful person!

GOD IS...

Read Psalm 18:3-4.
Blessing to be desired: a more
intimate relationship with God.

Your relationship with God is often revealed by the way you refer to God. Throughout your life, you probably addressed God by many different names depending on the circumstances of your life, how you saw yourself in relationship to God.

In the Hebrew Scriptures, when the Jewish people felt threatened by enemies they called God by such names as "a stronghold" (Psalm 9:10), or "King forever" (Psalm 10:16). When they realized their infidelity to God, they named God a "just judge" (Psalm 7:12). Later when they felt God's care and protection, they referred to God as "my shepherd" (Psalm 23:1).

In the New Testament Jesus refers to God many times as Father, while John says, "God is Light" (1 John 1:5) and "God is Love" (1 John 4:8).

Today, people use names for God that remind them of their experience of God. Some call God, "Friend," or perhaps, "Spirit of Life."

In your relationship with God what names have you used — in your childhood? in your adolescence? as a young adult? What is your name for God now?

Week Two
FOCUS ON GOD'S GIFTS TO YOU

The purpose of this week is to take a close look at some of the gifts God has given you and to realize more deeply how you have used these gifts. Before beginning your meditation be sure you are aware of God's presence. You cannot pray without this awareness, so take all the time you need to realize that God is near. If this takes the full 15 minutes on some days, do not be disturbed. No matter how long you wait, remember it is a great privilege to encounter God.

Again, suggestions for five meditations will be presented this week, allowing time for repetitions. Repeating a meditation is not the same as going over it again in the same way. Rather it is returning to particular points in the prayer that you found most fruitful. They may be attractions or insights that bring you closer to God. On the other hand, God can also speak through a negative reaction in prayer. A feeling of resistance or dislike for some point in the prayer tells you something about yourself or your relationship with God.

This repetition narrows the subject of your meditation to one or two points and allows the grace received through these insights to be deepened. Your mind will be less active as the ideas grow familiar to you and you will be freer to respond to God from your heart. It is good to return to these insights as often as you find it helpful.

Your notebook will help you locate these positive and negative feelings as the subject for a repetition. After each prayer jot down any thought, idea, or insight that may have attracted you or repelled you. Did you feel particularly happy, sad, joyful, angry or depressed after a meditation? Record these feelings. You might want to go back and discover why you felt that way during this prayer. If you felt that God was teaching you something in a meditation, return to that prayer and allow God to expand or reinforce that lesson.

The subject for your repetition does not have to be taken from this week's meditations. You may always return to a meditation from past weeks that was grace-filled for you. This is your retreat. Do not hesitate to use your freedom to respond in a unique way to God's call to you.

"HOW MARVELOUS ARE YOUR WORKS, O LORD!"

Read Genesis 1:1-25.
Blessing to be desired:
a love of creation.

As you read the story of creation let your imagination be filled with the abundance and overwhelming variety of God's creatures. Think of the vast number of different flowers, some so small they are hardly noticeable in the Spring grass, others with large, flamboyant blooms. Each one has its own beauty, its own glory to give to God. Each one speaks of God's presence in the world around you.

Look at the night sky. Even in the midst of city lights one cannot miss the myriads of stars filling the sky. Beyond the visible stars are the vast number of stars whose light has not reached earth yet.

As you marvel at the vast beauty with which God surrounds you, thank your Creator for these countless gifts of love. What do you say to God in response?

OUR CO-RESPONSIBILITY

Read Genesis 1:26-28.
Blessing to be desired: an awareness of our co-responsibility for the earth, air and water.

God crowned all of creation by making human beings in God's image and likeness and giving them the care of the earth and its environment, and all living things. Down through the centuries the world seemed so vast with such an abundance of plant and animal life that human beings lived in the illusion that resources were unlimited. We have failed to care for God's creation.

By making us aware of our destructive, wasteful habits, ecologists and environmentalists, like the prophets of old, are calling us to conversion. Reverence and love of God's gifts of creation can lead to taking the necessary steps to assume responsibility for our earthly home.

Ask Jesus how you are being called to reverence and protect the world he called "home" and that is now home to you.

GIFTED BY GOD

Read Matthew 25:14-30.
Blessing to be desired: to appreciate
your talents and abilities.

Besides all the gifts of material creation, God gives to each one certain individual gifts of heart, mind and body. One person may have an optimistic, happy outlook on life; another may have the gift of soothing troubled hearts; another has gentle, healing hands. Everyone has skills or talents which God expects that person to use in loving and serving others.

What talents has God given to you? Lovingly accept these gifts from your Creator. Enjoy your gifts and thank God for enriching your life in this way.

These gifts are not meant for you alone, for you to hoard and keep hidden. Be generous in using your talents to give others joy and loving service. As you use your talents, you are cooperating with God's action within you. Rejoice in the good you are doing with God.

FAITH

Read Luke 7:1-10.
Blessing to be desired: gratitude
for the gift of faith.

Jesus was amazed and delighted at the faith of the centurion. This Roman official did not have a Jewish heritage; he had not studied the Hebrew Scriptures. However, the Jewish elders were impressed by his goodness. He did not take advantage of his position but treated the conquered Jews with respect and love. His heart was open to the gift of faith.

No one can earn faith but it is a gift that God gives readily to those who are open to receiving it. Christians who are baptized as infants sometimes do not appreciate the tremendous gift they have received.

How have you treasured this gift in the past? Thank God for this priceless gift and ask for the grace to appreciate it more and more each day.

GOD'S MOST PRECIOUS GIFT

Read 1 John 4:14-16.
Blessing to be desired: a deeper realization and
experience of God's unconditional love.

God's gifts are different in some ways from the
gifts we receive from friends and family. A gift
from a friend is symbolic of deeper realities than
the gift itself. It tells us of the care, concern, and
love of the friend.

God's gifts are laden with spiritual power
for God is present in each gift. But God is not a
static God so the Holy One is also active and at
work in each gift. More wonderful than all other
gifts is God's unconditional love for each of us.

Let your heart be amazed at God's goodness and generosity. How do you respond to such
love?

Week Three
FOCUS ON YOUR EXPERIENCE

The meditations for the first week focused on how special you are to God and last week you realized more deeply some of the many ways God has gifted you. The meditations for this week continue to move in that direction. Their aim is to help you pray from your own experience.

You are very special to God. Therefore, everything you have done, everything that has happened to you, all your feelings and reactions to life's events — all that makes you you — is special to God. God was present in each moment of your life, in the good times and the difficult times.

Perhaps you were not aware of God's presence in these experiences. Now is the opportunity to relive past experiences and consciously share them with God. In this way you begin to see some of the events of your life as God sees them.

Allow those events to surface which God wants to bring to your awareness. As they come to mind try to see how the Holy One was present and respond to God. Let your response come from your heart, expressing to God your feelings as they arise in relation to a particular experience.

This kind of prayer allows you to be healed by God of any hurts, resentment, or anger that remain deep in your consciousness from past sufferings or disappointments. You can now be more joyful with God in the happy times, more grateful for God's strength and support in the difficult times, more repentant for the sinful times.

The goal of these meditations is quality, not quantity. That is, it is not important to pray about many experiences but to let God's presence in significant experiences touch you deeply.

Your prayer on the events of your past life will begin to affect your present life by making you more aware of God's action now. Your response to God will gradually become more wholehearted and loving. Even after the retreat is over you may want to continue mining the richness of your past life with God.

THE CHALLENGE

Read Luke 6:47-49.
Blessing to be desired: an appreciation
of the struggles in life.

Trees planted on a windswept hillside may lean with the wind but they are sturdy. Their roots dig deep into the soil, anchoring them firmly to withstand the gusts. A tree sheltered from the wind and storms is weak and easily uprooted.

Today as people live longer, they have come to recognize the importance of exercise and fitness programs. Muscles that are never used become flabby, and lose their tone and strength.

Teilhard de Chardin applied this phenomenon of nature to the life of the spirit. He wrote in *The Divine Milieu* that even if there had been no sin in the world we would have needed some challenge in life in order to strengthen our spirit.

Ask God to reveal to you how the challenges of your life have been opportunities to grow strong. Thank God for gifting you with opportunities to grow spiritually and emotionally through these challenges.

REJOICE!

Read Psalm 23.
Grace to be desired: a recognition of God's
presence and activity in your happiness.

At a time when life was very simple, the Psalmist pictures God first as a good shepherd and then as a generous host. In each image, God is the provider of all good things that bring happiness.

God provides for you directly in all the beauties of nature, the spiritual insights that come in prayer, the new life and strength given through the sacraments. God also showers you with happiness and grace through other people.

Ask God to bring to your mind several incidents from the past that gave you great happiness and joy. Savor these events, tasting again the delight of those moments. See God at work in these events that you may have taken for granted in the past. Now you have the opportunity to thank the Giver of all Gifts, and celebrate!

TAKE UP YOUR CROSS

Read Mark 8:34-36.
Blessing to be desired: to accept
the challenges of life as Jesus did.

You may be inclined to think of the cross of Jesus in a narrow sense — his suffering and death on Calvary. However, Jesus was challenged to carry his cross throughout his life. He suffered from the hostility of the scribes and Pharisees, the disbelief of his own people, the slowness of the apostles to accept his message, the misunderstanding of his friends, including his own mother. He experienced tiredness, hunger, heat and cold just as you do. These difficulties were the result of Jesus' fidelity to the Father. He continued to preach the Good News of God's love in spite of all difficulties. Jesus accepted his struggles and sufferings as the cross in his life.

To follow Jesus you do not need to look for hard things to do. You need only accept, as Jesus did, the sufferings and troubles that come into your life. Allow God to surface a few events from the past that were very difficult for you. Ask God to heal your heart as you see more clearly how God supported you with care and love. Thank God that these crosses made you a stronger person.

THE MERCIFUL FATHER

Read Luke 15:25-32.
Blessing to be desired: to experience
the mercy of God.

Jesus told this parable to highlight the mercy of God. Unfortunately through the ages, the younger son has received so much attention that both the father and the elder son fade into the background. The younger son lived riotously but the elder son was petty, whiny, jealous and ungrateful. He needed repentance and mercy too.

The purpose of meditating on sin is not to trigger guilt feelings but to realize more deeply the loving mercy of God. Like the father in the parable, God seeks you out and assures you of forgiveness and constant unconditional love.

How amazing and wonderful to realize that even in a sinful moment God loved you unconditionally and called you to receive your Father's loving mercy. As you reflect on sin in your life ask for a deep experience of the Father's merciful love.

A VISION OF LIFE

Read John 10:6-10.
Blessing to be desired: a share in
God's vision of human life.

In *Fully Human, Fully Alive*, John Powell writes that we all need a vision to find answers to life and to organize reality. Our vision gives direction to our behavior and is a frame of reference for responding to reality. Our vision tells us something about ourselves and the way we view other people and things in our lives. Usually our vision is not static, but can be changed if we want to change it.

One way to get in touch with your vision is to complete the statement, "Life is...." Or you might ask yourself, "What is the deepest desire of my heart?" It is this desire that influences much of your behavior, that is the driving force in your life. If this desire is operating at an unconscious level you may be a puzzle to yourself, finding it difficult to explain some of your attitudes and actions. This desire can be changed if you want to change it.

Spend some time in dialogue with Jesus about your vision of life.

Week Four
FOCUS ON YOUR DARK SIDE

The meditations this week continue to focus on God's gifts and your use of them. Several attitudes can be fostered and strengthened by meditation on God's gifts to you as an individual. One that many Christians forget is a sense of gratitude. It is human to beg God for our needs — and God wants us to offer prayers of petition — but a heart that neglects the prayer of gratitude is filled with false pride. Gratitude shows our recognition of our place as a creature and reflects an attitude of dependence on God.

Meditation on God's gifts also leads to a realization that we have not always used these gifts in an unselfish way. This realization should immediately call forth sentiments of sorrow and petitions for forgiveness. And God will answer our prayer with another gift: loving mercy.

The last meditation deals with an area of sinfulness that many Christians rarely consider. Since Vatican II, the Church has been calling our attention to sinful social structures which also need God's mercy. These structures are sinful because they keep some people in poverty and oppression, they foster racism and sexism, they condone injustices against the poor and minorities. As Christians we need to pray for justice and take whatever action we can to counteract injustice.

A prerequisite for understanding social sin is a realization that we all belong to one human family with God as our Father. As family members we need to be concerned that millions of people are living in sub-human conditions deprived of basic human rights. Our society is so complex, so interdependent that we cannot totally excuse ourselves of responsibility for the injustices in the world.

Considering the immensity of the task, we might feel very helpless. But as Christians we are called to pray and work for justice. We can pray that God's grace will touch the hearts of those with power to change oppressive structures. We can also beg the Spirit for light to see what we might do to foster peace and justice.

If you feel great resistance to admitting any responsibility for the evil in the world, beg God this week to open your mind and heart to the injustice around you. Ask God to reveal to you anything in your life that might contribute to the oppression or suffering of others. Just as God responds to repentance for individual sin by granting mercy and greater freedom, so will God respond when you repent for social sins and ask for forgiveness.

THE CONTRAST

Read Luke 5:4-10.
Blessing to be desired: to see
ourselves as God does.

Peter is suddenly struck by an insight that over-
whelms him. In contrast to Jesus, he sees himself
as "a sinful man," unworthy to be in the presence
of the Lord. He does not yet realize that Jesus
came to save sinful humanity.

Some people confess the same sin over and
over again for years without ever getting beyond
the outward action. They do not distinguish between a sin and inward sinfulness. Just as our
vision of life influences our behavior, so too a
sinful tendency can be expressed in many different ways. It is important for our growth in Christ
to discover our basic sinful tendency, the root of
sin in us. Then, with God's help we can hope to
be more like Christ.

THE SHEEP AND THE GOATS

Read Matthew 25:31-46.
Blessing to be desired: to see
sinfulness as Jesus does.

American society today has lost a sense of sin. Wrongdoing, even a serious crime, is often given psychological explanations, blamed on one's parents, neighborhood or friends. Few people want to admit that they have chosen to do wrong. It is even more difficult for many people to admit that their failure to do good can also be sinful.

In this parable, Jesus does not mention what we consider "big" sins. Instead he focuses on sins of omission, seemingly small things, like giving a cup of cold water to one in need.

Ask Jesus to reveal to you your attitude toward sin. Only God can give us a true sense of sinfulness and repentance, so different from guilt feelings.

SOCIAL SIN

Read Galatians 6:1-10.
Blessing to be desired: a sense
of oneness with humanity.

Watching the evening news on television, one might be overwhelmed by a sense of the evil in the world. There are reports of murders, rapes, drug addiction, terrorism, government scandals, business frauds — the list seems to go on and on. The temptation for good people is to think: "Aren't they terrible! How can they do such things!"

It is easy to forget that any sin is both individual and social. We are all involved in the evil in the world for we are born into a sinful world and we have added to the sinful environment in which others must live. Some of the actions we deplore on the evening news are a response to the unjust society in which we live.

Ask God to give you a deeper understanding of the way individual, personal sins affect others by adding to the sinfulness of the world. The evening news can be an opportunity to ask God's forgiveness and mercy on our society.

STEWARDSHIP

Read Luke 12:13-21.
Blessing to be desired: to listen
to God with an open heart.

God's gifts of creation are meant for all human beings to use. All have a right to a share in the good things of the earth to use in becoming a loving, serving person. When some people take more than their share, more than they can possibly use, others are deprived of their share.

Even a quick look at the world shows the inequitable distribution of the world's resources. The United States with 6% of the world's population uses over 40% of available resources. Ecologists are trying desperately to make us aware of the effect of our consumer society, calling us to be good stewards of God's gifts. Talk to God about this situation. Let God tell you what your response might be.

DISCERNMENT

Read Luke 2:25-28.
Blessing to be desired: the gift
of discernment.

Simeon lived his life in the presence of God. He could read the movements of his heart and knew when the Spirit was leading him. His faith was rewarded by holding the infant Christ and praising God for the salvation of Israel.

Discernment is the ability to notice the movements of our hearts, the ideas for action that pop into our minds. Then, through the power of the Spirit, we need to discover the source or motivation. We might be motivated by the Holy Spirit, our own selfish interests, or the evil spirit. What spirit is motivating me? Why do I feel drawn in this direction?

Discernment is a delicate, life-long process. It takes honesty and a sincere desire to know oneself as God does.

Week Five
FOCUS ON JESUS

The prayer for the remainder of the retreat will focus on Jesus. The goal is to encounter Jesus as he moved through his earthly life, to see how he reacted to the events of his life, to reflect on his values and to let those values permeate one's life. In this way the Christ-life that was received at Baptism grows and flourishes. The self-centeredness of one's life is replaced by the life of Christ, so that the Christian can come to say with Paul, "The life I live now is not my own; Christ is living in me" (Gal 2:20).

A few variations on the suggestions offered in the introduction will prove helpful in meditating specifically on the events of Jesus' life.

1) *Relax.* As in all kinds of prayer, the first step is to take a position that is comfortable and conducive to prayer. You have probably found from experience during the past weeks what position is best for you. Take this position and breathe deeply several times, letting the cares and concerns of the day slip away.

2) *Realize* that you are in Jesus' presence and ask him to let you share in this particular event of his life. Beg of him that all your

thoughts and actions, every movement of your mind and heart may give him praise.

3) *Read* the Scripture passage describing the event on which you are about to pray. Read slowly — seeing the scene, looking closely at the people, hearing the words that are said, watching Jesus especially.

4) *Try to place yourself in the scene.* Perhaps you can identify with one of the people present.

5) *Try to sense the way various people feel.* How does Jesus feel? What kind of response is he getting?

6) *Speak to Jesus* about your feelings and your response to this event. Listen to him.

You will find that if you can really become part of the Gospel scene you will react as yourself. You will take into the scene your own attitudes, hopes, fears, desires and prejudices. This type of prayer, therefore, can be the source of important insights if you reflect with Jesus on your reaction to the incident.

COME, LORD JESUS

Read Isaiah 11:1-9.
Blessing to be desired: that Jesus may
come more fully into your world.

Throughout Hebrew history, God kept alive the desire for the coming of the Messiah by sending prophets. Through the prophet Isaiah, God revealed some of the characteristics of the Messiah. He would be filled with the Spirit and would have a special concern for people on the fringes of society. He would establish a reign of justice and peace, a Kingdom free from violence and destruction.

The Jewish people longed and prayed for the coming of the Messiah. They yearned for God to save them from oppression, poverty and injustice.

You cannot pretend that Jesus has not already come, but you can enter into the longing of the Jewish people by desiring that God may be more actively present in your life.

You too can eagerly wait for Jesus to save people from the oppression of poverty and injustice still in the world. Pray that you may begin the meditations on the life of Jesus filled with an ardent desire to know him better, to love him more and to serve him with greater fidelity.

MARY'S "YES"

Read Luke 1:26-38.
Blessing to be desired: to respond
to God as Mary did.

Although Mary was very young, probably a teenager, she had a deep, mature relationship with God. Mary questions the angel about how she will become the mother of the Messiah, but she never questions or doubts God's will for her. She could not foresee all the consequences of her decision, but she trusted God. By saying yes to God she accepted all the responsibility and suffering that would come to her as the mother of Jesus.

At times, you may not understand where God is leading you. At such times it is important to pray to know God's will and to have the courage to follow it even though you do not know all the consequences.

Dialogue with Mary. Ask her to obtain for you the grace to respond to God wholeheartedly as she did.

MARY VISITS ELIZABETH

Read Luke 1:39-56.
Blessing to be desired: to enter
into Mary's song of praise.

After the angel left her, Mary was concerned about her cousin, Elizabeth. She did not consider the special privilege she had received as setting her apart from those who needed her. She set out immediately, walking though the hilly country to visit Elizabeth. God revealed to Elizabeth that the long-expected Messiah would soon be born, the son of Mary.

Mary responded to Elizabeth's joyous greeting with a hymn of praise to God. The hymn contains many phrases from the Hebrew Scriptures. At this time of great emotion, Mary praised God with the words closest to her heart, God's own words in Scripture.

Ask Mary to share in her joy and in her loving concern for others.

JESUS IS BORN

Read Luke 2:1-20.
Blessing to be desired: a sense of wonder
that God came to earth as one of us.

Through the yearly celebration of Christmas, we may become so familiar with the account of Jesus' birth that we lose the sense of awe for this mystery. Every newborn infant is a miracle of God's love. How much more, the Infant in the manger at Bethlehem. He created the world and now depends on Mary for everything.

Ask Mary to share with you the love and faith that filled her heart as she first looked upon her son. Or you might talk to Joseph as he marvels at the mystery of God's love. Or you might kneel beside the manger and speak to Jesus from your heart.

HUMILITY IN GREATNESS

Read Matthew 2:1-13.
Blessing to be desired: to recognize
Jesus in the poor.

The Magi represent all those who seek God with an open heart. They let nothing stand in the way of following the path God pointed out to them. When God no longer seemed to be leading them, they sought advice and counsel. They asked others to tell them where the Messiah was to be born. Because the Magi were so faithful, God manifested himself to them.

The Jewish leaders in Jerusalem had their own ideas about the coming of the Messiah. They were so certain of their own opinions that their minds were closed. John described them when he wrote:

"To his own he came,
yet his own did not accept him." (Jn 1:11)

Instead pagan philosophers from far away sought him and acknowledged in this little child the presence of God.

FOCUS ON JESUS' MISSION

Before beginning the meditations of this week it is well to review the introduction and suggestions for the fifth week. Take a few minutes to reflect on the meditations of the past week. Were they fruitful for you? Is there anything you want to change in your posture during prayer? In the time of prayer? In your efforts to realize God's presence? Check your journal. Are you jotting down significant reflections after your prayer each day? Make any changes necessary to help your prayer for the coming week be more meaningful.

The meditations this week are a bridge between the early life of Jesus and his public life. The incident in the Temple when he was 12 years old forms the link between his early childhood and his adult life. Luke concludes his narration of this event by remarking, "Jesus, for his part, progressed steadily in wisdom and age and grace before God and men" (Lk 2:52).

This one sentence is all the evangelists tell us of Jesus' life from the time he was 12 years old until he was moved by the Spirit to begin his public life. During all the intervening years he lived quietly doing the will of his Father by fulfilling the simple duties of a carpenter at Nazareth.

If we put high priority on activity, getting things done, seeing results, we might feel that these years were wasted for Jesus. The realization that Jesus "progressed steadily" by doing simple tasks in union with the Father's will helps us to set our priorities straight. He learned who he was and the meaning of his life. He developed all those qualities of mind and heart that made him fully human. Only by being fully human could Jesus redeem us in our humanness.

From this passage and other indications in Scripture, it seems evident that Jesus' human consciousness of himself as Messiah and Son of God was a growing awareness. He experienced a gradual clarification of his mission.

This week you will be asked to be with Jesus in incidents which bring into focus the mission to which he is called. As Jesus lived these incidents, his human experience of his mission grew and his dedication to the will of the Father was intensified. Try to enter into the spirit of this week with Jesus.

JESUS FOUND IN THE TEMPLE

Read Luke 2:41-51.
Blessing to be desired: the grace to
ponder God's touches in your life.

After fulfilling their obligation to worship in the Temple at Jerusalem, Mary and Joseph began their journey back to Nazareth. At nightfall they realized Jesus' absence.

Jesus felt a strong attraction to remain in the Temple where faithful Jews found the presence of God in a special way. Apparently, Jesus was beginning to realize something of his mission from God. He sought to clarify his call among those who seemed to know God's ways best.

Returning to Nazareth with Mary and Joseph, Jesus realizes that God's time for him to begin a public mission has not yet come. God's will for him was to grow in wisdom and grace.

We can never be absolutely sure of God's will for us. After careful discernment, we move in the direction God seems to indicate, trusting that God will continue to lead us. If God's ways seem contradictory or mysterious, we need to praise the wisdom of God as we admit our human limitations.

THE BAPTISM OF JESUS

Read Matthew 3:13-17.
Blessing to be desired: an increasing
awareness of your baptismal life.

Even though Jesus was sinless and therefore had no need for a baptism of repentance, he chose to enter the baptismal waters to associate himself with sinful humanity. This was a further step in clarifying his mission: he was sent to liberate us from sin.

The words, "This is my beloved Son," echo Isaiah 42:1 and identify Jesus as the Suffering Servant mentioned by Isaiah. In the prophet's vision the Messiah was not to be a powerful, wealthy leader but a poor and suffering servant.

Through the Sacrament of Baptism, we share in the life of Jesus. His values and characteristics should shine forth from Christians carrying on the mission of Jesus.

THE FIRST TEMPTATION

Read Luke 4:1-4.
Blessing to be desired: the attitude of
Jesus toward material things.

In the baptismal scene, Jesus appears as the Son of God, sent by the Father to bring all people into the fullness of the divine life. In the temptations, it becomes clear that Jesus is also fully human.

Jesus is led by the Spirit into the desert for a time of prayer to clarify his mission. How is he going to carry out God's will for him? How is he going to attract people so that they hear God's message?

The bread represents material things of all kinds. Jesus is tempted to attract people by using his power to give people everything they need or want for their physical life. Jesus answers this temptation by stating that his mission is concerned with life that goes beyond the physical.

The devil still tempts people with the desire to possess and accumulate many things in order to distract them from caring for their inner life.

Talk to Jesus about your priorities.

THE SECOND TEMPTATION

Read Luke 4:5-8.
Blessing to be desired: to avoid manipulation
in dealing with others.

In the second temptation the devil puts before Jesus a vision of all the political domains of the world. Again this temptation questions what kind of Messiah Jesus will be. Will he use power and force to get people to follow him?

In his answer, Jesus acknowledges that God alone should receive homage and adoration. He is putting his mission under the will of the Father. He will preach the Kingdom and appeal to human faith and love. People must be free in their response to him and in their relationship with God.

Anyone who wishes to join Jesus in spreading the Kingdom must also present the message without coercion or manipulation.

Speak to Jesus about his mission and how you can share in it in a non-manipulative way.

THE THIRD TEMPTATION

Read Luke 4:9-13.
Blessing to be desired: that the example of Jesus
may be a source of strength in time of temptation.

Luke presents Jerusalem as the setting for the third temptation just as Jesus' entire ministry was a journey to his death in Jerusalem. The devil suggests that Jesus attract people by using the spectacular. This would have been an easy way to gain followers, but Jesus knew that salvation must come through faith which is always humble and often involves suffering.

Luke remarks that the devil left Jesus for a while "to await another opportunity." These other encounters between Jesus and Satan are more evident in Matthew's Gospel.

Through his death and resurrection Jesus won complete victory over Satan and the power of evil. St. Paul says that we are called to share in the glorious heritage of Jesus and "the immeasurable scope of his power in us who believe" (Ep 1:19). In the power of Jesus' resurrection we can be victorious over any temptation.

Week Seven
FOCUS ON THE KINGDOM

The goal of this week is to hear the call of Jesus asking you to help spread the Kingdom. The message of Jesus in the Gospels is that God's reign is both now and yet to come. Jesus established the Kingdom when he was here on earth but its complete fulfillment will not take place until the end of time when all things are united in Jesus and returned to the Father.

Listening to Jesus preach about the Kingdom, the people in the audience were excited by the Good News. This is what they had been waiting so long to hear.

Today, when many Americans hear the word "Kingdom" they react negatively. It seems to contradict the American ideal of democracy. However, the concept Jesus was announcing might also be expressed in other ways without even using the word "Kingdom."

Jesus calls each of us to cooperate with him in carrying out the plan of the Father that all people hear the Good News, accept it and rejoice with the Father forever. The message of Jesus involves liberation and reconciliation — liberation from the bondage of sin and reconciliation with the Father and with one another.

Besides the outward thrust toward others,

the call of Jesus at this point in your retreat is a challenge to you to grow in deeper identity and intimacy with him. If you are to share his work you must first share in his life. As the retreat progresses it will become clearer to you how you can share in the life of Jesus. For now, it is enough to respond wholeheartedly to Jesus in an open-ended way, trusting that he will show you the way during the remaining weeks of the retreat.

JOHN'S MESSAGE

Read Matthew 3:1-3.
Blessing to be desired: to understand
more clearly the mission of Jesus.

John was sent by God to help people prepare their hearts for the imminent coming of the Messiah. By announcing "The reign of God is at hand," he holds out the hope that God will soon intervene in history in a new way. In order to recognize this new action of God, people must first examine their lives. Then they must reform, that is, change anything that might be an obstacle to their acceptance of God's action.

Each Ash Wednesday we hear again John's message of repentance calling us to change our lives. If we respond positively we can look forward to a new intervention of God in our lives as we celebrate new life with Christ at Easter. How has God intervened in your life in the past? Thank God for these interventions and clear your heart for God's action in the future.

THE TIME OF FULFILLMENT

Read Mark 1:14-15.
Blessing to be desired: to hear with
enthusiasm these words of Jesus.

After his prayer and fast in the desert, Jesus is ready to begin his public life. Now his mission is so clear to him that he can state it in concise terms. He knows exactly the good news that he must preach to the people. He reiterates John's theme but then announces that God's promise is being fulfilled NOW. What tremendous news! Their waiting is over. "This is the time of fulfillment!"

This was a turning point in history. Human history would never be the same for all of humanity is called to believe the Good News and manifest that faith in daily life.

Every individual must make a response. Each of us can say, "Today is the time of fulfillment. How will I reform my life, believe and live the Good News?"

GOD'S REIGN

Read Matthew 13:33.
Blessing to be desired: to radiate the joy of
God's presence and action in your life.

Jesus wanted the people to understand God's reign so he told a simple parable. Like leaven in dough God's reign is within and radiates outward. It grows within a human heart and spreads from there to other hearts. Just as the yeast spreads throughout the dough until the whole is leavened, God's reign is spreading gradually throughout the world.

A Christian who is sharing in God's life should radiate joy and a sense of inner peace. Without saying a word such a person witnesses to a presence within that attracts others.

Think of the people who have influenced you; did you sense this inner radiance that spoke of God's presence? Thank God for his presence among us and offer to do your part in spreading the Kingdom.

KINGDOM VALUES

Read Matthew 5:1-12.
Blessing to be desired: a firm resolve
to make these values your own.

The Beatitudes are values of the Kingdom. They are the ideals that will become a reality when God reigns completely in his world. The poor in spirit, the meek, the pure of heart, those who thirst for justice —all will know God's presence; he will reign in their hearts.

The Beatitudes present values contrary to the Jewish values of Jesus' time. Certainly they oppose present-day values of wealth, self-assertion, competitiveness and status. In order for God to reign more completely in human hearts, one must be willing to take on the values of Jesus as expressed in the Beatitudes.

Share with Jesus your honest reaction to his values.

YOUR KINGDOM COME

Read Matthew 6:7-13.
Blessing to be desired: a longing for the coming
of the Kingdom in its completeness.

In this brief prayer Jesus reveals to us the petitions
we should include in our prayer. Jesus shows us
what is important — spreading the Kingdom. It is
clear that our spreading the Kingdom is associated with doing God's will.

At any moment God is aware of all the
events that make up the world. In that same
instant, God envisions all the possibilities for
moving the world toward the fulness of the Kingdom. God offers these possibilities to human
beings, attracting and luring them to cooperate
with him in this creative work. Depending on the
response, God adjusts the vision of an ideal world
to the new situation and presents new possibilities for our cooperation. When we cooperate
with God's work in the world we are doing God's
will. In the process we become the true selves
God intended us to be.

Rejoice in the good, the true and the beautiful that God and you are bringing into the world.
What a wonderful privilege to cooperate in God's
action!

Week Eight
FOCUS ON JESUS' PUBLIC LIFE

The meditations for this week and next will center on the public life of Jesus. From the very beginning of his life Jesus was identified with the marginalized of society. He lived most of his life in Nazareth, a place so insignificant that Nathanael could voice the popular opinion of it: "Can anything good come from Nazareth?" (Jn 1:46). Until he was approximately 30 years old Jesus was a simple carpenter. Even the Nazarenes questioned where he got his learning since they knew him only as a carpenter (Mk 6:1-3).

As Jesus began his public life he deliberately chose to be associated with those who were rejected. He began preaching in Galilee, a section of the country that was considered unimportant, marginal to Jewish life. At his baptism he chose to identify himself with sinners. He walked along the sea of Galilee and chose ordinary fishermen to be his first disciples. His first miracle was performed for a poor couple who could not afford enough wine for their wedding. He talked to a Samaritan woman — that despised people — and revealed his identity to her. He preached about a Kingdom in which those who are rejected by society are welcomed.

Sinners, the poor, the oppressed, the outcast are all given special attention and love by

Jesus. This preference of Jesus for the poor makes one wonder: If Jesus appeared on earth today, where would he be preaching his message?

To be a true follower of Jesus, one must take on the values of Jesus. As you see Jesus associating with his favorite people, let his attitudes, his values permeate your heart until they become your own.

As Paul wrote to the Philippians, "Your attitude must be that of Christ" (2:5). Taking on the mind and heart of Jesus, being motivated by his values, one then becomes ready for discipleship.

Discipleship means living in the service of the Kingdom. This not only means the doing of good deeds for others — although this is certainly one aspect of service. Rather, serving the Kingdom means bringing the message of Jesus to others. The giving of self to those in need — consoling the sorrowful, bringing comfort and hope to the sick and suffering, striving for justice for the oppressed — makes the message credible.

As you share with Jesus these events of his life ask him how he is calling you to more dedicated discipleship. How can you in your uniqueness participate in the dynamic saving mission of Jesus?

THE FIRST SIGN

Read John 2:1-11.
*Blessing to be desired: an appreciation
of the role of Mary in the Church.*

John tells us that "Jesus performed this first of his
signs at Cana" (2:11). A sign is more than simply
one miracle among many. John uses the word
here in its fullest possible sense: a sacrament, an
outward sign that leads to faith and a recognition
of the presence of God. As a result of this sign,
Jesus' first disciples believed in him. Jesus still
works through signs, the sacrament which ini-
tiates us into faith, Baptism, and those which
increase our faith and life with God, especially
the Eucharist.

After the Resurrection, Mary assumes a new
role as Mother of the Church and, as such, she is
concerned about each of us just as she was
concerned for the young couple.

Try to become part of the scene at Cana.
Listen to the dialogue between Jesus and Mary;
watch the action take place. Talk to Mary about
her part in this event; about her concern for you
and her care of the Church.

THE SELF-RIGHTEOUS

Read John 8:2-11.
Blessing to be desired: to be healed
of any self-righteousness.

The sensitivity and compassion of Jesus are very evident in this incident. The story highlights the respect and concern that Jesus had for women. His attitude contrasts sharply with that of the scribes and Pharisees who brought the woman to Jesus. Forgetting their own sinfulness, they were only too ready to stone her. (There is no indication, however, that the man involved was threatened with the same fate.)

By turning away from the accusers and marking in the sand, Jesus made the scribes and Pharisees face their own sinfulness. They who were so eager to judge and punish another could only slink away with their own burden of guilt. Jesus does not condone the sin of the woman but he is gentle and forgiving.

Perhaps the most subtle temptation of good and holy Christians is the tendency to be judgmental and self-righteous. Real discernment is necessary to be aware of self-righteous judgments.

THE SAMARITAN WOMAN

Read John 4:4-18.
Blessing to be desired: the
courage of an open heart.

Hostility between Jews and Samaritans was so intense that many Jews did not risk traveling through Samaria. Jesus not only goes through the country but cuts through all taboos by speaking to a Samaritan woman. It was unheard of for a Jewish rabbi to talk with a woman in public, but Jesus was not influenced by the prejudices of his time toward women.

Jesus was aware of the kind of life she had led but he saw the good in her: her openness to his message and her desire to find God. Jesus uses water as a symbol to teach her about the life he has come to share with us. The water Jesus gives is a fountain within a person, bubbling with eternal life.

We have received this life in Baptism. Like all life it must be nourished and fostered in order to bubble up and overflow on the world.

AN ENTHUSIASTIC DISCIPLE

Read John 4:19-42.
Blessing to be desired: to share the enthusiasm
of the Samaritan to spread the Good News.

The Samaritan woman shares with Jesus her faith in the promise of the Messiah and her readiness to believe that "when he comes, he will tell us everything" (4:25). She receives in return, Jesus' revelation, "I who speak to you am he" (4:26). How thrilled she must have been to hear these words!

When the disciples returned, the woman rushed off to tell her experience to anyone who would listen. Many did listen and came to hear the Good News from Jesus. Later, when the townspeople were somewhat complacent in their faith, the woman must have smiled to herself, for she knew they had come to Jesus because she had spread the Good News.

Recall times when you have spread the Good News. How did you feel? Rejoice in those events and thank God for the opportunities.

CREATIVE FRIENDS

Read Mark 2:1-12.
Blessing to be desired: trust in
the goodness of Jesus.

The ingenuity of the paralytic and his friends is matched only by their faith. Seeing their faith, Jesus first forgives the man's sins and then cures him. By forgiving his sins Jesus makes it very plain that health of soul is far more important than health of body.

The paralytic was not embarrassed to use whatever means necessary to find healing. As he was lowered through the roof he was not thinking about what people would say about him. His one thought was to approach Jesus with his need.

Through the Sacrament of Reconciliation and the Eucharist, health of soul and strength to lead a new life are available to us. Sometimes we too must be creative in finding opportunities to approach Jesus through the sacraments. Speak to Jesus about your appreciation and use of the sacraments.

Week Nine
FOCUS ON COMMUNITY

The meditations for this week continue with incidents from the public life of Jesus, but the focus is on some broader areas of Christian living. As Jesus feeds the crowd, you will reflect on the nourishment you receive in word and Eucharist, a community experience. You will be asked to examine how you give witness to your faith and how you hear Jesus' call to service.

We all need the sense of belonging, the encouragement and support that come from being part of a Christian community. For many people the natural communities of family and neighborhood groups have been shattered, leaving feelings of loneliness and alienation. Some look to the parish but soon discover that its very size makes it almost impossible for a real community to form. It is a rare parish where the people really feel a bond of union with one another at the Sunday Eucharist and are alive to the fact that they form a worshipping community. As the people of God, as Church, we need to shake our apathy and ask ourselves, "What can I do to help form a Christian community?"

Each of these meditations should move you to reflect on your relationship with Jesus in the midst of others. The Christian life can never be a private affair between one person and Jesus. It must necessarily be lived and experienced in a mutual interaction with others that is both challenging and life-giving. If your prayer at this time tends to be too much "Jesus and I" make a conscious effort to broaden your vision. Try to share the loving concern that Jesus has for all human beings.

Several of these meditations ask you to reflect with Jesus on the faith he expects of his followers. It is important to keep in mind that faith is not primarily a belief in a creed but an acceptance of a person: Jesus. To accept Jesus totally may be frightening, for that means we also accept his values, his total dedication to the will of the Father and his way of life. By ourselves this total acceptance of Jesus would be impossible. The Father gifts us with faith; we show our gratitude by continually begging for an increase of faith.

THE FAMILY OF JESUS

Read Mark 3:31-35.
Blessing to be desired: an appreciation and love of all the members of God's family.

The "brothers" of Jesus mentioned in this text are generally thought to be his cousins or other relatives. Jesus is not rejecting his ties to his family but indicating that there are bonds uniting individuals which go deeper than family relationships. Those who do God's will are united to Jesus and to one another in the family of God. God's reign (and his larger sense of family) may make demands that take priority over natural ties with family, relatives or friends.

Being a Christian and belonging to the family of God is a constant challenge. Ask Jesus for a vivid realization of your place in God's family. Talk to him of the challenges you experience in doing God's will. How have you been helped by the other members of God's family?

THE PROMISE OF SPIRITUAL FOOD

Read Mark 6:34-44.
Blessing to be desired: a deep hunger
for the Eucharist.

When Jesus heard of the death of John the Baptist he withdrew to a deserted place along the shore of the sea of Galilee. This place was not too far from several cities and the people came out looking for him. He was moved by compassion for the people for they "were like sheep without a shepherd," needing guidance and leadership. He saw their need and responded to it.

Although they were in a deserted place, the people could have gone to a nearby town or village to purchase food. But Jesus preferred to feed them himself, using gestures that anticipated the institution of the Eucharist. He provided food for their physical nourishment; he would soon give himself as food for our spiritual nourishment. Jesus nourishes our spiritual life through the bread of the Eucharist and also the bread of his Word.

Speak to Jesus about your eagerness for the bread which nourishes your spiritual life. Do you hunger for Jesus and search out opportunities to be nourished by him?

THE STORM AT SEA

Read Matthew 14:22-33.
Blessing to be desired: a strong faith
that does not falter at challenges.

Jesus went to the mountain alone to pray. This is one of many Gospel scenes that depict Jesus praying to the Father. Because he was human as well as divine, he needed to spend time with the Father in intimate, personal prayer. You might want to spend the time of this meditation on the mountain with Jesus praying to the Father.

In Christian art, the Church is often symbolized by a boat. It may be shaken by troubles and difficulties, but Jesus is never far away, even though he is invisible. As Church, we can count on Jesus being nearby no matter what storms we encounter. In order to keep from making the same mistake Peter made, we must keep focused on Jesus.

The successor of Peter and other Church leaders have many responsibilities and cares. They especially need our prayers for a steadfast faith. They also need our cooperation and our loyalty.

Talk with Jesus about your feelings of Church. Ask him for help never to let petty differences weaken or polarize your local Church.

THE POWER OF FAITH

Read Mark 5:25-34.
Blessing to be desired: faith in
the healing power of Jesus.

In Mark's Gospel, the healing power of Jesus seems to have an almost magical quality. Mark makes it clear, however, that Jesus is responding to the faith of the woman. It seems evident that the miracles of Jesus had some effect on him. Each one was a draining experience; he felt power going out of him.

Often those who minister in Jesus' name find themselves called upon to meet the needs of more and more people. Like Jesus they feel drained of both physical energy and spiritual resources. It is consoling at such times to know that Jesus had the same experience. We should recognize that Jesus is calling us to spend some time alone with him to allow him to strengthen and refresh us.

Like the woman who touched Jesus in faith, approach Jesus seeking the healing you need in spirit, mind or body. Present your needs to him simply, trusting in his power and in his love for you.

MARTHA AND MARY

Read Luke 10: 38-41.
Blessing to be desired: a heart that
discerns its Martha-Mary role.

Martha and Mary symbolize two aspects of our relationship with Jesus. There are times when we need to sit quietly with Jesus and listen to his words. At other times, we must serve him in the poor, the suffering and the helpless.

Jesus does not expect frantic, over-eager service that leads to frustration, exhaustion and anger. Our service should be characterized by an awareness of God's presence in those we serve, leading to calmness and poise.

Neither does Jesus expect long, isolated prayers and endless devotions. Jesus led a balanced life of prayer and ministry and expects us to do the same.

The light of the Spirit is needed to know when and how much one should minister to others, when it is time to withdraw for prayer and quiet, and when to relax and have fun. We cannot minister nor pray well with a tired, run-down mind and body.

As you pray for a discerning heart, ask Jesus to show you how to achieve in your life that balance which he desires.

Week Ten
FOCUS ON JESUS' PASSION

Your prayer for this week will center on those special proofs of his love which Jesus gave us during his passion and death. The passion of Jesus is always a fruitful source of meditation; some saints have spent years meditating on Jesus' sufferings and his love for all people.

The focus in these meditations is the death of Jesus as an expression of his love for the Father and for us. The emphasis is not so much on what is being suffered as on who is suffering and why. In praying about the sufferings of Jesus, each person can truly say, "Christ suffers all this for my sins." For one who is a follower of Jesus, the only appropriate response is: "What can I do for him?"

The suffering and death of Jesus calls us to reflect again on sin, for it is sin that brings Jesus to the cross. The cross reveals not only the seriousness of sin but the depth of the Father's love and mercy for us. By taking up the tiny crosses of our daily life we can enter into the suffering of Jesus. Then our suffering, like his, becomes redemptive. Accepting suffering does not take it away, but it does give meaning to the difficulties of life.

Even in our suffering we must realize that God does not directly will suffering, that is, he does not cause it. Suffering comes because of evil in the world. Therefore we must constantly struggle to overcome evil. Our best efforts are limited and may prove futile, but we can still draw good from suffering by uniting it to the suffering of Jesus.

As in previous weeks, five meditations are presented for this week. It is most important that you feel free to choose whatever part of the Passion will be most helpful to you. You might want to spend the first day's meditation reading the Passion in all four Gospels and choosing passages for your prayer during the remainder of the week.

THE INSTITUTION OF
THE EUCHARIST

Read Luke 22:14-20.
Blessing to be desired: a deep appreciation
and love of the Eucharist.

Try to be present in the Upper Room to celebrate
the Passover with Jesus and his apostles. It was at
the ritual blessing of bread and cup that Jesus
consecrated the bread and wine. Then he told his
apostles, "Do this as a remembrance of me" (Lk
22:19). In the context of the Passover meal remembrance means more than mere recollection.
In this ritual remembrance it is God, not just
people, who remembers. In so doing he makes
present the great acts of redemption. So at each
Eucharist, we do not look back in memory to the
Last Supper; the Last Supper is made present to us
so that we may experience the saving power of
Jesus. Each Eucharist should be approached with
faith and awe.

John does not include the institution of the
Eucharist in his Gospel account. Instead he nar-
rates the washing of the apostles' feet by Jesus.
Jesus' lowly service shows us how the Eucharist
should change our lives from self-centeredness to
humble service of others.

Tell Jesus what the Eucharist has meant to
you in the past; what it means to you now. How
are the effects of the Eucharist evident in your life?

THE AGONY IN THE GARDEN

Read Mark 14:32-42.
Blessing to be desired: a realization of the
presence of God in times of darkness.

As he had done so often during his life, Jesus wanted to spend some time alone in prayer to the Father. He was faced with the climax of his mission. The "hour" had come, the time of his suffering, death, and glorification. Jesus felt human repugnance toward suffering, but even in his distress and fear he was perfectly in tune with the Father's will. Even in his agony, Jesus knew God as his Father and expressed his trust and his willingness to accept the Father's will until the end.

The attitude of Jesus was in sharp contrast with that of the sleeping disciples. At the moment of deepest confrontation between Jesus and Satan, Jesus prayed. The disciples too must encounter Satan, but they slept on, not even aware that the "hour" had come.

Try to be present with Jesus in his sorrow. There will be times in your life when it will be difficult to accept God's will for you. Ask Jesus to help you draw strength and support from his prayer and agony.

PETER'S DENIAL

Read Matthew 26:69-75.
Blessing to be desired: steadfast fidelity
to God in every difficulty.

Peter — the Rock — is an example of human weakness. As a close follower of Jesus, he knew he was putting himself in great danger when he went into the courtyard to be as near Jesus as possible. His courage failed him just as Jesus had predicted. Peter denied even knowing Jesus.

Peter did not conceal his weakness; neither did he try to condone or justify it. "He went out and began to weep bitterly" (Mt 26:75). He is not only an example of human weakness but, more importantly, an example of heartfelt repentance.

Peter teaches us that we are all weak and need to pray for courage to be faithful to God. If, or when, our courage fails us, we look to Peter's example of immediate, sincere repentance.

JESUS CARRIES HIS CROSS

Read Luke 23:26-30.
Blessing to be desired: a
compassionate heart.

As Jesus carried his cross through the streets of Jerusalem, women tried to console him. Jesus tried instead to comfort them because of the sorrows that would come upon Jerusalem.

Mary was probably among the women at the side of the road.

Through the centuries Mary has been the strength and consolation of countless women who have had to watch their children suffer, for she knows the desire of a mother to take upon herself the sufferings of her child.

It is not necessary to look for extraordinary ways to follow Jesus. The cross, for most people, consists of all the frustrations, irritations, difficulties and troubles that can — and do — intrude into daily living. The willing acceptance of these problems in order to be like Jesus is carrying one's cross in the footsteps of Jesus.

Be with Mary by the side of the road. Speak with her about her feelings then and your feelings when you see an innocent person suffer.

JESUS DIES ON THE CROSS

Read John 19:25-30.
Blessing to be desired: letting go
of self-centeredness.

St. Paul wrote about Jesus: "Though he was in the form of God, he did not deem equality with God something to be grasped at. Rather, he emptied himself and took the form of a slave, being born in the likeness of men" (Ph 2:6-7).

During Jesus' passion and death, the emptying process continued as he was stripped of everything that human beings value. His friends betrayed or deserted him; his own people rejected him and demanded his death; his reputation was gone as he was sentenced to the death of a common criminal. Through all of this, Jesus clung to his Father's will.

Hanging on the cross, Jesus saw at his feet two people very dear to his heart; his mother and his beloved disciple, John. Desiring to be stripped of everything, he gave them to each other. With nothing left on earth and realizing that "everything was now finished" (Jn 19:28) he gave over his spirit to the Father.

In spirit, kneel at the foot of the cross and speak to Jesus from your heart.

Week Eleven

FOCUS ON THE RISEN LIFE OF JESUS

As you approach the end of the retreat, be open to share in the joy of the first disciples at the Resurrection of Jesus. It seems somehow easier to be compassionate with Jesus during his sufferings than to rejoice with him in his glorification. And yet the sign of a Christian should be the joy born of the conviction that Jesus has truly conquered sin and death for us. His victory is our victory too.

The Resurrection affirms for us that suffering and death are not the ultimate realities. As God's love triumphed in the Resurrection of Jesus, his love will also triumph as we pass through death to new life. This is the foundation of our faith, for as Paul tells us, "If Christ was not raised, your faith is worthless" (1 Cor 15:17). With this solid foundation the Christian can face suffering and death with hope, trust, and even joy, knowing that victory is near.

The Resurrection narratives reveal to us in a special way the consoling Christ. He appeared to the weeping Mary, to the fearful apostles and to the confused disciples on the way to Emmaus. To each he brought peace and the joy of his presence. Seeing Jesus in these events helps us to realize that he is truly present even in his apparent absence.

As you pray do not be concerned if the Resurrection narratives seem somewhat disconnected. The details do not follow in a neat and orderly fashion; they reflect the excitement and rejoicing of the disciples. The accounts of the first Easter morning especially give the impression of much confusion in the news about the risen Lord, of a great deal of running back and forth from the Upper Room to the tomb.

Do not be too concerned about details, about an orderly arrangement of appearances. Try to get in touch with the excitement, the joy and amazement of the first Easter morning. Try to identify with one of the persons in each narrative and to experience his or her feelings as that person realizes Jesus truly lives.

"HE IS NOT HERE"

Read Luke 24: 1-12.
Blessing to be desired: a share in
the joy of the Resurrection.

In spite of their fear the women went to the tomb at dawn on the first day of the week. They were the first to receive the good news that Jesus had been raised up and was indeed living. Into hearts still filled with grief, confusion and fear, joy began to penetrate — joy tempered by the fact that they had not yet seen Jesus.

The apostles reacted to the news of the women with an attitude of male superiority. "The story seemed like nonsense and they refused to believe them" (24:11). Peter at least went to see for himself and came away amazed but still not knowing what to believe. That Jesus had been raised from the dead as he had promised seemed too good to be true.

Try to enter into the mixed emotions of the women — their fear, confusion, and then the joy of realizing that Jesus lives. Open your heart and let Jesus share with you the joy of his Resurrection.

THE HUMOR OF
BEING HUMAN

Read Luke 24:13-27.
Blessing to be desired: the ability to share
God's humor and laugh at yourself.

Luke mentions "two of them" (24:13), that is two
of Jesus' disciples. They may have been a man
and his wife returning to Emmaus after celebrat-
ing the Passover in Jerusalem. They were disap-
pointed and saddened by the events of the past
days. In their depression they hardly noticed the
stranger who joined them on their journey.

Later, as these two disciples recalled the
irony of their explaining to Jesus what had happened to him, did they laugh at themselves? Only
the humble of heart can admit their human
limitations and laugh at the times when they took
themselves too seriously.

Recall some time in your life when Jesus
might have said to you, "What little sense you
have!" Are you able to see the humor in your
reactions and laugh with Jesus as together you
talk over this event?

WITH BURNING HEARTS

Read Luke 24:28-35.
Blessing to be desired: the ability to recognize
Jesus as he accompanies you on your journey.

When the disciples arrived home they invited and urged the "stranger" to remain with them. Jesus gladly accepted their invitation and responded by revealing himself to them.

Jesus never forces himself on anyone. He will not stay where he is not wanted but always accepts an invitation to be with you. At times it is difficult to see that he is present; you may not recognize him. At other times you will be filled with joy as you recognize him "in the breaking of the bread" (24:35).

Thank Jesus that he is so available, so ready to accompany you in your daily life and so desirous of giving himself to you in the Eucharist.

PEACE

Read John 20:19-23.
Blessing to be desired: the reconciling
peace of Jesus.

To complete the joy of the Resurrection, Jesus appeared to the disciples as they gathered in fear behind closed doors and gave them his Spirit and reconciling peace. Even today, whenever a person is reconciled to God or to another person, there is a renewed presence of the Spirit and the peace of the Risen Jesus.

We wonder sometimes how we can help to bring peace to a world in conflict. If there is to be peace among nations there must first be peace among those who call themselves followers of Jesus. Until reconciliation takes place there can be no experience of peace.

Ask Jesus to look at your relationships with you. It is not always easy to become reconciled with someone who has harmed you. It is not easy to let go of the anger and resentment and to treat that person with the kindness of Jesus.

Is there anyone with whom you need to be reconciled? If so, ask Jesus to go with you to make peace with this person. He will give you the courage to say what is necessary. He will be the bond of peace between you and the other person.

"DO YOU LOVE ME?"

Read John 21:15-19.
Blessing to be desired: a
wholehearted love of Jesus.

Jesus gives Peter an opportunity to witness to his intense love for him before the other disciples. There must be no shadow of a doubt in the minds of the disciples that Peter, in spite of his triple denial, loves Jesus intensely. In order to strengthen Peter's position as head of the Church, Jesus even foretells that Peter will die for him.

Jesus addresses to you the same question he asked Peter, "Do you love me?" As you respond to Jesus, assuring him of your love, hear his command: "Feed my lambs... Feed my sheep." Love needs to find expression in service and ministry in the name of Jesus. How can you express your love for Jesus in the future?

Week Twelve
FOCUS ON BECOMING A FORERUNNER

You have reached the last week of your retreat, a week of integration and listening for the call of Jesus to carry on his work of spreading the Kingdom. In the meditations for this week you accompany the disciples to the mount of the Ascension, and then wait with them for the coming of the Holy Spirit. They go forth in the power of the Spirit to proclaim the Good News.

Eugene La Verdiere, in his book *When We Pray...* points out that it is not enough to be a disciple. Disciples are learners and must be ready to take an active role by becoming followers. In his Gospel, Luke always uses the verb form, "those who follow" in order to emphasize how we must become active in the service of Christ.

Having taken on the values of Christ, you may sometimes be called to become a forerunner. Even as far back in history as the time of Isaiah, eight centuries before Christ, forerunners prepared the way for the arrival in an area of an important person. Isaiah writes of the coming Messiah:

"In the desert prepare the way of the Lord!
Make straight in the wasteland a highway for our God!

Every valley shall be filled in,
every mountain and hill shall be made low;
The rugged land shall be made a plain,
and the rough country, a broad valley.
Then the glory of the Lord shall be revealed,
and all mankind shall see it together,..."
(Isaiah 40:3-5)

If God's Kingdom is to be fulfilled, Christians today must prepare the world for the revelation of Christ. Many of the values in our society are contrary to the values of Jesus as we find them articulated in the Beatitudes. Hearts must be prepared to hear the Good News. This is your challenge as you complete this retreat.

THE ASCENSION

Read Acts 1:6-9.
*Blessing to be desired: strong faith in
the presence of Jesus among us.*

Luke began his account of the early Church with
a brief summary of the time between the Resurrection and Ascension. Even after the Resurrection the apostles did not fully understand the
mission of Jesus for they asked, "Lord, are you
going to restore the rule to Israel now?"

The apostles had already received the Holy
spirit on Easter evening, but Jesus promised a
further outpouring of the Spirit to give them
power to witness in his name. Jesus commis-
sioned the apostles to spread the message throughout the whole world.

How lonely the apostles must have been at
first until they realized that somehow Jesus was
still with them. Talk to Jesus about your experience of his presence in your life.

WAITING

Read Acts 1:10-14.
Blessing to be desired: patience
to wait for God.

This passage describes what might be considered the original support group. The disciples, along with Mary and the other women, had experienced the death, resurrection, the puzzling appearances of Jesus, and then his departure from them. All these experiences created a bond between them as they returned to Jerusalem to await the promised coming in power of the Spirit.

Going to the Upper Room, they had no indication how long they would have to wait, but they "devoted themselves to constant prayer." They talked to God and to one another about the meaning of their common experience. Their waiting was not a sterile waste of time but a deepening of their understanding and faith.

We too need to take time to pray and reflect with people who have had experiences similar to our own. This shared reflection gives new insight to all in the group and strength to face new challenges in life. Talk to God about your experience of faith communities. Thank God for the gifts you have received through such a group.

DESCENT OF THE HOLY SPIRIT

Read Acts 2 :1-13.
Blessing to be desired: gratitude for the work
of the Spirit in your life and in the Church.

The power of the Spirit was manifested through the powers of nature — loud wind and fire. All those in the room participated in a powerful spiritual experience as a community. All received the same Spirit. But this was also a personal, individual spiritual experience for the tongues of fire came to rest over each one. Each one received special gifts from the Spirit so that together they could nourish and expand the infant Church.

The apostles realized that their gifts were meant to be shared and immediately went forth to speak God's word to those gathered in the streets. The Spirit was also active in the peoples of many lands, opening their ears to hear the Good News.

Ask God for a share in this Pentecostal excitement and joy. Think about how you might use the gifts the Spirit has given you for the good of others.

THE EARLY COMMUNITY

Read Acts 4:32-37.
Blessing to be desired: that modern communities
may share the values of these early communities.

Luke's account of the early communities seems
like an ideal, too beautiful to be true. We see the
Beatitudes in action as these early Christians
loved and cared for one another. In the first fervor
of their new-found faith they show us that living
the Beatitudes is a possibility. These are the
values we need to work toward in our parishes
today.

However, Luke also shows us the other side
of early community life — the lies (5:1-11), the
arguments over accepting the Gentiles, the selfish-
ness when they gathered for the Eucharist, etc.
These accounts too are lessons for parishes today
— attitudes and behavior that erode community
life.

As you come to the end of this retreat, how
are you moved by the Spirit to help your parish
incorporate the positive values of the early communities? Talk with God about what you can do
for your parish.

THE SPIRIT AT WORK TODAY

Read Romans 8:18-27.
Blessing to be desired: to grow in your ability to
see the Spirit at work in your life and the world.

Today scientists are becoming aware of the inter-dependence of all creation, a truth which Paul wrote about two thousand years ago. Human beings and all living things are united in their struggle against the consequences of sin in the world. All of creation will be fulfilled in Christ when redemption is complete.

The rest of creation depends on human beings for we are the only ones who can choose. We have the Spirit living within us to guide us in our choices. As Paul tells us, left to ourselves we would not know how to pray nor what to ask of God. The Spirit prays within us and our Father understands our halting words. Let the Spirit lead you in a prayer of praise to God for all of creation. Thank God for all the gifts you have received and especially those known only to the Spirit.

THE CLOSING MEETING

As you come together to share on the meditations of last week, you may want to spend some time reflecting on the retreat experience. As you look back over the weeks, does some special grace stand out? Can you find a golden thread or pattern running through the entire retreat?

It is well to bring an experience of this kind to closure rather than letting it just stop. One suggestion for closure might be to prepare a small table with candle, flowers, and open Bible around which you gather. After an appropriate song, those who wish might share what the retreat has meant in their lives, followed by the *Our Father* and St. Ignatius' *Prayer of Offering.*

Ignatius' Prayer of Offering

Take, Lord, receive all my liberty
My memory, understanding, my entire will.
Take, Lord, receive all I have and possess.
You have given all to me;
Now I return it.
Take, Lord, receive, all is yours now;
Dispose of it wholly according to your will.
Give me only your love and your grace;
That is enough for me.

CONCLUSION

You may find yourself at this point asking, "Now what?" Some retreat groups have agreed to continue meeting to pray together and share faith. Mark's Gospel may provide a good springboard. The narratives are short, action-filled incidents in the life of Jesus. By reading the account slowly it is relatively easy to identify with one of the participants and enter the scene. Perhaps another part of Scripture appeals to your group. Using Scripture as the background for prayer has several advantages:

1) As the Word of God, it is a very effective way for God to speak to our hearts.
2) It is a never-ending source of insight, for it tells of God's activity in human history.
3) It keeps your prayer fresh by providing a different aspect of life for meditation and prayer each day.
4) It enriches your relationship with God.

After your prayer each day, make a brief notation in your prayer journal. This habit developed during the retreat can be a source of many insights in the future. Go back to the meditations where God was especially present to you and relive the graces of those moments. If there were times when you experienced resistance, take the opportunity to encounter these barriers and seek the root of your resistance.

One last suggestion: In your search for a deeper relationship with God in your daily life, you might find a spiritual director can be very helpful. Someone trained in spiritual direction can give you encouragement and support in your journey to God.

This book was designed and published by St. Pauls/Alba House, the publishing arm of the Society of St. Paul, an international religious congregation of priests and brothers dedicated to serving the Church through the communications media. For information regarding this and associated ministries of the Pauline Family of Congregations, write to the Vocation Director, Society of St. Paul, 7050 Pinehurst, Dearborn, Michigan 48126 or check our internet site, www.albahouse.org